# FORGED

Shaped, Strengthened, Sharpened:
A journey in spiritual refinement

By

Danielle Downing-Hadley, MSS, LSW, M.Div.

Unless otherwise indicated, Scripture quotations taken from the New American Standard Bible® (NASB),

Copyright © 1960, 1962, 1963, 1968, 1971, 1972, 1973, 1975, 1977, 1995 by The Lockman Foundation
Used by permission. www.Lockman.org

Copyright © 2018 Danielle Downing-Hadley.

All rights reserved. No part of this publication may be reproduced, distributed, or transmitted in any form or by any means, including photocopying, recording, or other electronic or mechanical methods, without the prior written permission of the publisher, except in the case of brief quotations embodied in critical reviews and certain other noncommercial uses permitted by copyright law. For permission requests, write to the publisher, addressed at the e-mail address below.

ISBN: 978-1-7353608-0-5 (Paperback)

Book design by Kanitra Alston.

First printing edition 2019.

Danielle Downing-Hadley
ddowninghadley@yahoo.com

## Dedication

*This devotional is an offering unto my Lord and Savior Jesus Christ. To my family, may you always be refined by our Father.*

## Forward

I am so honored to write this forward for one of my spiritual daughters who is such a phenomenal person and is so dear to me. Her teaching has had a profound impact on my life. She has inspired me because of her unwavering commitment to be scholarly and her profound passion to be intimate with the Lord for her to receive revelatory insights. The Lord has gifted Danielle to be multifarious and yet she has maintained a humility that is authentic and one that is not disingenuous.

Danielle serves in our church in various capacities. She is an integral member of our ministerial staff, she serves as our youth pastor along with her husband and she is the dean of our bible school. Danielle has a servant's heart, she is a critical thinker that has insights and perspectives that challenge us to think outside the box.

Knowing that Danielle has a heart to see believers become intimate with their Savior and to be "shaped", "strengthened", and "sharpened" until they are conformed to the image and likeness of Jesus; I am not taken that she has masterfully put together a plan that would help them on that journey.

This seven week devotional will challenge you to deal with not only knowing who you are but will help you to become more intimate with the One who chose you and has a plan, purpose and a design for your life that will allow you to be what He has destined you to be in Him.

Forged is a blueprint to help you get from where you are and to help you get closer to where you need to be. For this to happen, one must be open to self-introspection, honesty, transparency, authenticity, humility and a desire and willingness to allow the Holy Spirit in places in our lives that need healing and refining.

This seven-week devotional is not designed to be the ultimate answer. The journey of refinement is not done in seven weeks or for that matter seven years, it is a journey for life. This devotional will get you started on the journey and then you will have to decide how long and how committed you will be to the process of God's forging and refining. The good news is, if you commit to the process, you can rest assured that He who began a good work in you will be faithful to complete it.

In His Refinery,
Bishop Michael Brokenborough

## Introduction

The process of spiritual refinement is one that begins with a basic understanding not only of God and who He is but also your relationship with Him. It is my hope that this book will assist the reader in dedicating time to intentional personal intimacy with God through prayer and understanding the biblical significance of the refining process. This book is a 7-week devotional and should be used daily for maximum benefit. Forging, the process of sword making will serve as a metaphor for the spiritual sharpening that is a process of refinement. It is important to note that this is only a metaphor used to illustrate a complex and often arduous process. While there are many measures for evaluating a sword, generally the four key criteria are hardness, strength, flexibility, and balance. These elements can also be used to evaluate Christian life and will be representative of the refinement which we seek.

## Week 1

### What kind of metal?

In the process of sword making, the first step is selecting metal or metals to be used to craft the final product. Metals are selected in various amounts for their strength, quality, flexibility, and purity. At the onset of this journey of refinement we must remember, we have been handpicked by God for His plans and purposes. Like an artisan selecting materials this selection process occurs with little or no intervention from us. We do not have input on how or why God selects us. This week, we will focus on reminding ourselves of who we are and whose we are; in other words, we will rest in the fact that God's plans for our lives not only supersede our own but are also intentional. It is imperative that we acknowledge our inability to craft ourselves outside of God's will. We can, however, submit our will to God and allow Him to fashion us for optimal usage in His kingdom.

## Day 1

*You did not choose Me but I chose you and appointed you that you would go and bear fruit and that your fruit would remain, so that whatever you ask of the Father in My name He may give to you. - John 15:16*

Today's reading is a simple acknowledgment of the fact that despite humanity's best efforts when left to our own devices we do not choose God. We do not start the process of refinement rather we join in the process by submitting to the will of God. God's selection of us is completely dependent on Him, not us!

Therefore, it is God who does the work of perfecting us, shaping us, molding us and preparing us to bear fruit. It is not enough to know that this is a fact. We must rest in the belief that if God has chosen us of His own will and His own accord, He has found us useful. Many Christians spend far too much time on what they consider deficiencies. Spending time ruminating on lack is not profitable and can lead to stagnation in spiritual growth.

In doing this we become trapped in either low-self-esteem or false humility and potentially remain in a state of stagnation due to our perceived inadequacies. This is not a position that is profitable for us and such a position will not lead to spiritual refinement. As Christians we do not have to do anything, fix anything or improve anything for God to love us or use us. God has been aware of our faults, flaws and shortcomings from before the foundations of the world and He chooses us with that knowledge. He chooses to use us not because of who we are at first glance, but He sees us for who we can become in Him. In Him we can become more then we could every fathom because it is God who reveals our true substance. He has intentionally chosen us for whatever "metal" we contain. It is God's job, not ours to bring about our final purpose.

*Lord today and every day let me rest in your choosing. Let me be willing to engage in the process of sanctification. Let me trust in your ability to cause even barren trees to flower. I can bear a plentiful harvest and I wait for you to bring it to pass.*

## Day 2

*There is no one who calls on Your name, Who arouses himself to take hold of You; For You have hidden Your face from us. And have delivered us into the power of our iniquities. But now, O LORD, You are our Father, We are the clay, and You our potter; And all of us are the work of Your hand. - Isaiah 64:7-8*

We are the works of God's hand. Today, let us be reminded that in Him our greatest potential can be realized. Just as a potter shapes the clay, you are the product of God's divine design. Every nook and every cranny of your inner being is not only known to God but is also purposeful. Nothing about you surprises God, nothing about you is disqualifying and God is ever still working on you to create a magnum opus. Many of us have come from sordid or shameful pasts that can plague us with negative thoughts and insecurities. When we look through this lens our vision is obscured. Many people operate in filtered thinking or cognitive distortions based upon negative input from the environment. We then evaluate ourselves only by our moral failures. We look at what we cannot do rather than what we can do.

God does not use the same measuring tape or criteria that we do. God never measures us to something or someone else, rather He equates us to us. We do not have to achieve another person's pinnacle of success in God's eyes. We need only measure up to our own potential. Our goal should always be to achieve God's plans and purposes for our own lives. In other words, God knows who we are and who we can become in Him. God looks at our intended purpose and evaluates us based on His plan and purpose for our lives. He looks at the problem we have been created to solve. God knows that we are the answer to another person's question. Today let us be reminded that our process is God initiated, God sustained, and ultimately God completed.

*Lord, let us be reminded that you look at us in a way that sees beyond our own perceptions. Remind us that your opinion is the only one that matters. Let us not seek validation from anyone but you. Let us not look to the left or the right but let us only look to you. You are our strength.*

## Day 3

*Blessed be the God and Father of our Lord Jesus Christ, who has blessed us with every spiritual blessing in the heavenly places in Christ, just as He chose us in Him before the foundation of the world, that we would be holy and blameless before Him. In love…- Ephesian 1:1-4*

Knowing that we are chosen should be enough to cause us to rest in the will of the Lord, however, most times it is not. We must embrace the fact that God's choice is the only one that matters. We are often plagued by our own internal mantra which recounts countless negative comments and rehearses our spiritual and moral failings, but we must combat those attacks with the truth of God's word. God choose us long before we could be qualified for any position He destined for us. We need not concern ourselves with deficiencies that we see with our own eyes.

You are so vital to God's long-term eternal plans that He chose you before the foundation of the earth that you walk upon.

Embracing this truth with the entirety of our hearts is the foundation of our confidence in the awesome power of our God. It is not enough to know the facts of the matter, rather we must rest in the truth. Truth is something that surpasses our ability to rationalize or comprehend. Truth is not subject to our whims, our plans or our opinions, therefore, it is not based on our feelings or perceptions.

The truth is that we have been blessed beyond measure just to know God and experience His matchless love. The truth is we do not always know how, when or why God chooses, however, the act of God choosing validates us. The truth is that we are not lowly or deficient because we are seated in heavenly places. He chose us! He chose you! Now go walk in it!

*Today let us rest in the Lord. Let us be reminded that You chose us long before we had any value. You chose us in your divine wisdom without care of defects, deficiency or disrepair. You, Lord in your infinite wisdom have blessed us with every spiritual blessing and desire that we walk in your destined assignment.*

## Day 4

*For by grace you have been saved through faith; and that not of yourselves, it is the gift of God; not as a result of works, so that no one may boast. For we are His workmanship, created in Christ Jesus for good works, which God prepared beforehand so that we would walk in them. - Ephesians 2:8-10*

It is easy to forget that we are not saved only from something, but we are also saved to something. In other words, the same grace that God offers at the time of our salvation is the very same grace we must offer ourselves and others. Understanding that grace is a multifaceted concept that implies God's willingness to offer a gift humanity could never earn or deserve therefore, the criteria is not based on our performance.

It is not uncommon to question God's plans because we are judging ourselves far too harshly. Do not forget that we are the workmanship of God. The very same God who crafted the sun, moon, stars, planets, the heavens, earth and the entirety of the universe is the same God that is crafting you. He crafts with purpose, intention, and detail. The most poignant thing is that His crafting is not contingent on anything that we do or need to do! Just as we cannot earn more grace, we cannot alter or change God's design for our lives as long as we are walking with Him and remaining in His will.

Know that God's ultimate design for you is for your good. His design is not to harm, hurt, or humiliate. No matter how it may seem in the natural, all of God's crafting is intended to bring about brilliance, radiance, and joy not only for you but for those around you. We must learn to rest in God's skillful and deft hands and not be consumed by our own thoughts or estimations. We must learn to trust that God's plan is far greater than any plan no matter how splendid we could craft on our own.

*Lord, let me learn to trust in your awesome, amazing and abundant love for me. Let me not fear that your plans for me are too big, too vast, too challenging or out of reach. Today, remind me how much you love me. Remind me Father of the great sacrifice you made so that I might have access to eternity.*

## Day 5

*For I know the plans that I have for you,' declares the Lord, 'plans for welfare and not for calamity to give you a future and a hope. Then you will call upon Me and come and pray to Me, and I will listen to you. You will seek Me and find Me when you search for Me with all your heart. - Jeremiah 29:11-13*

This is a passage that is quoted often but the context is not routinely explored. God is having a conversation with His prophet explaining to him that the time for exile has come. God tells Jeremiah of the calamity, horrors, and displacement that his kin is about to endure. The Israelites are going into exile, a place that is unknown and God is telling them (not just Jeremiah) that He is not abandoning them. He is reassuring them that He is a God of redemption and the end of their journey will not result in their destruction but will end with goodness. In this passage it is important to recognize that God does not rescue His people from going into exile in the first place. It is crucial to examine the human desire to escape tough times and hard situations. It is natural to want to take the easy way out of hardship or conflict. We want to be rescued from our uncomfortable circumstances, but it is the more difficult times which produce character and define excellence. Like the nation of Israel in this passage, we are required to go through hardships either of our own doing or by God's design. Hardships can be used to bring people together.

Difficulty can cause one to seek the Lord both collectively and as individuals. We are driven to seek after God. We search for Him and when we find God amid our struggle, we find that we have not been abandoned. This scripture is evidence that we are never left alone, God is committed to our process. He has a plan to bring us to a place of expectancy and prosperity.

*Lord on this journey, I ask that You open my eyes to the plan that You have for me. I ask that You not let me be deceived by the way my life circumstances make me feel. Let me trust only in Your plan. Remind me that Your plans are good and that You will not abandon me or the plan that You have for my life.*

## Day 6

*"But He knows the way I take; When He has tried me, I shall come forth as gold. "My foot has held fast to His path; I have kept His way and not turned aside. - Job 23:10-11*

People naturally tend to look for a way out of tight situations. We do not like to be uncomfortable for long periods of time. Sure, we can withstand certain pressures of life when we can see that the result will prosper or enrich us in some way. For example, it is easier to work every day when you know there will be a paycheck at the end of the week. It is also easier to diet and exercise when there is an outfit that you must fit into by a certain time. This tangible, ever present reminder of the end goal helps push us past our discomfort toward progress. However, when we cannot see the benefit of the discomfort, it is even more difficult to remain still through the process of refinement. God's process guarantees a stronger and more fortified outcome than any earthly process we could endure. We will not always be able to discern the spiritual value of the things we will have to go through. God knows each twist and turn that our lives will take. It is not a surprise to Him. He knows the beginning and end of our journey, each hill, each valley, every plateau and every mountain top is familiar to our Father. He has the spiritual equation which we have very little ability to comprehend until after the transformation has taken place. Humankind's inability to perceive the spiritual equation makes it difficult for some to surpass discomfort while refinement is taking place. I encourage you to keep moving forward as the reward is at the end of your testing period; those that quit in the middle will not be able to experience the brilliance that comes forth as gold.

*Lord, You have a plan. You know the way I take; You will not lead me astray. What You have for me is for me and I will rest in your plan. No matter what I see with my eyes or feel in my heart, I will choose to trust Your plan above my own.*

## Day 7

*...fixing our eyes on Jesus, the author and perfecter of faith, who for the joy set before Him endured the cross, despising the shame, and has sat down at the right hand of the throne of God. - Hebrews 12:2*

The process of being forged, being shaped, being refined is one that requires intensity and pain. It is ultimately a faith walk. Like chiseling a smooth stone into a carved work of art, God allows us to be bruised, battered and chipped away. He allows this to illustrate His magnificent glory. In these moments, it is imperative that we know that God is perfecting our faith. He has not abandoned us rather He is the one who is all around us while we are being shaped. This process of refinement is not at all easy, it is not glamorous, and it is not to be taken lightly. The process is difficult and might cause us great consternation. We may be angry and confused but ultimately, we must trust that God is doing what He promised. He is perfecting us. This process is the very same process Christ endured for our salvation; therefore, God is not oblivious to our plight, yet it is necessary for us to endure our crosses to become the work that God intended.

Our plight brings not only glory to God but also blessings for us, precisely because God is the perfecter of our faith. To reap the benefits of faith, we must first learn how to withstand the test and trials of life. This fact is not contingent on how we feel now nor does it matter how difficult it may seem now. Faith in its nature is transformative. Faith is not stationary as we mature our faith in God grows also. We must acknowledge that faith is required for our walk with the Lord. Our faith is being tested and refined at each level of growth. We must be mindful that our persistence will be rewarded if we press on toward our Christ given goal.

*Lord God allow us this day to be reminded that You are the one who is perfecting our faith. Let us rest in the fact that your method is uniquely tailored and designed for us. You know exactly what You are producing in us. Help us to remain focused on Your perfect plan for our lives. Let us be renewed and refreshed through this knowledge and let it carry us through the process.*

Week 2

**Forging**

Forging is the process by which a bar of a desired metal or combination of metals is heated in a forge. The resulting material is then hammered into shape. This long and intentional process is enacted by the sword maker and it morphs the physical properties of the metal being crafted. This process that is repeated throughout the process of sword making heating, hammering, cooling and heating again is done in order to perfect the final product. This is done to keep the desired properties of strength and flexibility over the original metal.

This process also happens in our spiritual refinement. The Lord gathers all that is in us that is good, useful and desirable. He places us into situations that will purge us of those things that are not like HIM. The mindsets, behavior patterns and relationships that draw our hearts away from Him he will then purge in the refiner's fire. Many erroneously believe that when negative, painful or devastating things occur in our lives it is the work of Satan, however, many times this is not entirely true. God can ultimately use any situation that we encounter for our good. His plans supersede any plan of the enemy.

The forging process looks different in the lives of individuals, but the result is the same. God allows heat to both strengthen and purify. In this process we can grow weak as greater heat and pressure is applied. Therefore, we must look to Him for our strength through this fiery process.

## Day 1

*"O Nebuchadnezzar, we have no need to answer you in this matter. If that is the case, our God whom we serve is able to deliver us from the burning fiery furnace, and He will deliver us from your hand, O king. But if not, let it be known to you, O king, that we do not serve your gods, nor will we worship the gold image which you have set up." - Daniel 3:16-18*

There are times when we as the children of God are called to go into the fire. Generally, we are not excited by the prospect. It is natural to desire to stand far away from anything that will cause us to be purged. This is the challenge of the believer. We are in a position to be tested, not only through tangible physical means but also spiritually. This dichotomy between physical and spiritual often happens in tandem. At times we may only see the physical aspect of our refinement; it comes in the form of stress, distress, lack of finances, anxiety, oppression, and rejection. During refinement, do not get stuck focusing only on what is happening to you, but on what is happening in you spiritually through your circumstances. Every fire in your life that God allows has a purpose.

The young Hebrews had no guarantee that God was going to rescue them from the flames but as their statement points out they were confident that He was indeed able to do so. In times of intense situational heat be reminded that God can intervene on our behalf and if He chooses not to that does not make Him any less powerful. Our God can rescue us at any given point but there are times in life where the experience of the fire produces something so great that you must be willing to be kissed by the flames to encounter it. Beloved, do not run from the flames, your willingness to stand is not only a benefit to you but a testimony to those around you.

*Lord God, I know that Your plans for me are not to harm me. I know that Your plans are designed to bring life, brilliance, and excellence. I know Lord that Your refinement process is one that is crafted in love and though I may feel the flames of the fire I will not be consumed. I will emerge without even the hint of smoke. Help me today find peace in Your process.*

## Day 2

*For You have tried us, O God; You have refined us as silver is refined. You brought us into the net; You laid an oppressive burden upon our loins. You made men ride over our heads; We went through fire and through water, Yet You brought us out into a place of abundance. - Psalm 66:10-12*

Being tried, tested and refined is not easy. It is erroneous to think that we will float through this process like leaves on the calm surface of a still pond. While there are moments in this journey where we will be afforded rest and solace, be mindful that refinement requires a whittling down of frivolity. We are being pressed, being placed in dicey situations and being required to endure various levels of discomfort and pain. This passage of scripture reminds us that our pain is not ignored and unnoticed by God. The Lord in His infinite wisdom knows the end from the beginning; He can give us abundance after we have been stripped. To purge us of all that is the antithesis of what God desires, we must endure the heat and intensity of the forge. We are emptied of all that may hinder us on the journey ahead. We cannot always see what God is doing. We may not approve of how God is doing it. We may lose loved ones, wealth, security, employment or a host of other physical or emotional things. Peace can only come if we are cognizant that God promises us restoration. Once we have been depleted, we can then be restored.

Notice that both fire and water have been highlighted in the passage because though they are the opposite of each other, refinement needs both water and fire. Fire and water can destroy but they also have the capacity to cleanse, purify and bring renewal. As the Lord brings these elements together know that it is a necessary part of your being crafted and drawn ever closer to Him.

*Lord God, there are many times when I question the refinement process. I ask that You continue to hold my hand as I journey through dry arid places. The fire is hot, but I know that it is meaningful and necessary for my strength and resilience as a believer. Do not allow my courage to fail.*

## Day 3

*Therefore, they inquired further of the LORD, "Has the man come here yet?" So the LORD said, "Behold, he is hiding himself by the baggage." - Samuel 10:22*

In this passage it is interesting to see the man that God has anointed king hiding among the bags. The passage gives us little insight regarding why Saul is exhibiting this seemingly bizarre behavior. In the passage and in common culture bags are symbolic of the past. There are all types of baggage we carry around, emotional baggage, psychological baggage and baggage we carry from traumatic events. No matter how cumbersome this baggage is we can grow accustomed to it over time. Paul was comforted by the old things in his life. Saul was uncomfortable with the foreign new thing that God was doing in his life. It could be that this man of God was hoping that the lot would not fall on him or that by some strange inexplicable circumstance, God had made a mistake or suddenly changed his mind. Perhaps Saul was being humble or maybe he was just being scared. Just a moment ago Saul was searching for some lost livestock and now he is assigned to lead an entire nation of people!

There are many times in life where the assignment appears so vast and so heavy that it would be easier to "hide in the stuff" than attempt to fulfill the mission. Remember: If you can do it in your own strength, the task requires no faith. If you have the power to bring it to pass, then God has no part. Works of the flesh do not qualify as the promise of God. God calls us to perform 'mission impossible" because He alone makes the impossible, possible!

It does not behoove us to waste valuable time and mental energy ruminating our inadequacies. God not only knows where we struggle but can use us intentionally despite our ineptness. To bring Him glory and cause others to look not to us but to the God of our salvation.

*Father God, I may not always have a clear vision of why You chose me. Today, I will trust that no matter my past you are orchestrating my future. Lord, nothing is impossible and in You, I can do all things. No matter the vastness of the task!*

## Day 4

*"And I will bring the third part through the fire, refine them as silver is refined, And test them as gold is tested. They will call on My name, And I will answer them; I will say, 'They are My people,' And they will say, 'The Lord is my God.'"* - Zechariah 13: 9

This passage of scripture has a deep rich meaning in Hebrew culture however as Christians we can use this passage to see God's heart for refinement. In this example we can see God's delight to refine us. He does not perform this action without intention. God loves us so much that He is willing to journey with us on this path and through this process. Just as with Israel, God also gives us an opportunity to return to Him after we go astray. When a person comes into the family of God they are seen through the blood of Christ which absolves them of sin. However, this does not mean that one becomes impervious to the desire to sin. Sanctification is a process that occurs as one is being refined. We may be tested and tempted by our desires. Going through the fire is not pleasant; it burns, it singes, it scorches however, this passage reminds us that God does not leave us alone in the midst of this process. Though the answering of our many questions may not come in the form that we desire, it does indeed come.

Refinement places us in a posture of prayer. When one is being stretched and pulled within an inch of breaking is it the natural inclination of the soul to call out to the One that made it. Just as this passage suggests, difficult and trying times push us into the arms of God. It is these times we learn how to communicate with God on a deeper level. Prayer that is intentional, pure and genuine is birthed in times of trial and testing. Our prayers will not be left unanswered, we will not be abandoned because we are the people of God. We will never be alone.

*You are my God. I am nothing without you. In you, I find my meaning and my purpose. As gold is tried and tested, I will be tried and tested but because I am yours you will not allow the fire of refinement to consume me. I will emerge brilliant and resilient, ready to war for you.*

Day 5

*Not that I speak from want, for I have learned to be content in whatever circumstances I am. I know how to get along with humble means, and I also know how to live in prosperity; in any and every circumstance I have learned the secret of being filled and going hungry, both of having abundance and suffering need.*
*- Philippians 4:11-12*

During times of intensity or hardship, it is easy to get sucked into feelings of self-pity, despondence or depression. This happens when we focus on all the seemingly negative circumstances that are befalling us. Those types of feelings mean that we are looking at the wrong thing, focused on the wrong facts and distracted from the true value of our suffering. If we take a moment to reevaluate our position by finding a point of gratitude, our mood may shift. Having gratitude for what we have rather than lamenting all the creature comforts we may lack is integral in refinement. We must learn to desire not only what feels good but what is good for us in our process.

This is one of the first steps to examining the world with the mind of Christ. When Jesus looked at the fish and the loaves on more than one occasion. He asked: "What do we have?" rather than asking how many people needed to be fed.

It is this type of thinking that leads to acceptance and contentment. It is this attitude of appreciation that begins to permeate situations and circumstance making the process of spiritual refinement a little less arduous. Being content with your life and learning how to accept the process of shaping required to bring glory to God is not only imperative but an act of worship. Finding a moment of gratitude, no matter what situation befalls you is a sweet fragrance unto God. Gratitude centers you and realigns your focus on God. Being grateful is the bedrock of peace and the fountain of joy flows out of the believer.

*Lord, I ask that you help me today not to focus on all that I do not have. I ask that you remind me of what I do have. I pray that you will soften my heart and open my eyes to see the beauty in even the most unpleasant situations. Remind me that not every day is stormy and that rainbows only appear after rain.*

## Day 6

*... that they would seek God if perhaps they might grope for Him and find Him, though He is not far from each one of us; for in Him we live and move and exist, as even some of your own poets have said, 'For we also are His children.' - Acts 17:27-28*

It is easy for the believer to say with their mouths that they are essentially nothing without God. Those that have experienced a time when they did not know or acknowledge the presence of God have lived in spiritual isolation. Finding the love of God has a profound impact. The believer clings to God with every fiber of their being once they have found Him precisely because they know what it is to live without Him. During times of great trials, there can arise a moment of despair, what some theologians call the 'dark night of the soul'. This occurs when we are unable to see the resolution of our pain and suffering. This phenomenon is one can potentially happen to everyone who confesses Christ. Our searching and groping for God does not end when we find Him. This process of continually seeking God is essential to life. It is through this seeking and finding that we indeed live, move, and have our being. It is part of what it means to be a follower of Christ. We must be willing to go through the fire, again and again, to seek and find, to pursue the things of God no matter how elusive. It is true that He is never far from us but the act of seeking, searching and submitting to His divine will for our lives is what builds faith and character in the life of the believer. Just as the act of repeated heating and cooling creates a stronger and more battle-ready sword, the process of seeking after God, finding Him and then seeking again produces a believer who knows how to hear the voice of God. They know how to pray, to worship and war all because they are relentless in their pursuit of God.

*Lord increase my passion for You, increase my desire to seek Your presence. Allow my worship to be pure, intentional and without limits. Let my soul delight in seeking your face, not for Your blessings but just to be close to you. You are my father and I am your child.*

Day 7

*My soul, wait in silence for God only, For my hope is from Him. He only is my rock and my salvation, My stronghold; I shall not be shaken. On God, my salvation and my glory rest; The rock of my strength, my refuge is in God. Trust in Him at all times, O people; Pour out your heart before Him; God is a refuge for us. - Psalm 62:5-8*

The definition of the word refuge is a condition of being safe or sheltered from pursuit, danger, or trouble or something providing shelter. As we navigate our life's journey, God is our refuge and our refuge is in God. This simple statement is profound; we often seek refuge from the troubles of life forgetting that God is and always will be our place of refuge. God is bigger than any problem, obstacle or circumstance we may encounter. Our hope should lie securely in Him. No matter what wars rage around us, He is our rock. We must not be shaken or disconcerted by what occurs during our journey. When we place our trust in God it affords us the opportunity to ensure the outcome will be to our eternal benefit.

 Salvation is no longer an issue; death is no longer an issue because on the cross Jesus settled the matter for all eternity. Therefore, in our refinement, we can honestly pour out our hearts in its entirety before the Lord. Sometimes we may find ourselves only revealing part of our heart to God. We fear that He might reject us if we were honest about who we truly are, but this voluntary unmasking is the goal of refinement. During this process, we reach a point where we can be naked, bare and truthful not only with God but also ourselves.

Nothing about us will cause God to reject us and we trust that in our walk with the Lord He accepts us where we are, as He crafts us into what He wants us to be.

*Lord, we acknowledge that You are our source. Not in what we can fashion or secure on our own. Our will is swallowed up by Your will and we will choose to trust Your plans by any means necessary.*

Week 3

**Annealing**

When the forging process is finally completed, the sword has been purged and hammered into its final shape. The resulting sword is then heated and allowed to cool very slowly. The entirety of the sword is then wrapped in an insulating material to slow down this cooling. This process is called annealing. It is intentionally slow to set in place all the work that has been prior to the annealing process. If the sword cools too quickly the resulting product can be so hard that any further work could produce cracks or fragments. Such a sword would be ill equipped to handle the latter stages of sword creation. By annealing the metal beforehand, continued work can take place without any risk of cracking, as annealing releases mechanical stresses produced during machining or grinding. Annealing creates a material that is strong yet soft and easy to grind.

Using this as our analogy, we will utilize the concept of resting in God for the next seven days. When you have been heated, battered and stretched, it is imperative to take time to rest in the Lord. During the 'cooling' process it is necessary to focus on the moment you are in right now. It is not beneficial to get lost in the past or be so obsessed about that future that we forget the present. Being intentional about staying in the moment, mediating on the goodness of the Lord, worshiping in various ways all direct our attention to God rather than to our circumstances.

Resting can be challenging in a culture that demands busyness and productivity. Finding moments of peace and rest is not optional. Just as our physical bodies will shut down without proper rest so will our emotional and spiritual nature. To rest in God is to honor Him. Though it may be challenging it is our purpose this week to rest in His loving arms.

## Day 1

*Unless the LORD builds the house,*
*They labor in vain who build it;*
*Unless the LORD guards the city,*
*The watchman keeps awake in vain. - Psalm 127:1*

We live in a culture that is obsessed with production. We are taught as children that working diligently and wholeheartedly will produce better results than laziness. While this assertion is not completely incorrect, this idea can produce a generation of people that rely solely on their own abilities to get things done. We begin to do first and ask for guidance later. We do a work then ask God to bless it rather than inquiring of God before we move. Why does this matter you ask? It matters because of the essence of today's scripture. Those that create without the guidance of the Lord, produce monuments to themselves. They gain recognition for themselves and they do not direct glory and honor to God. Laboring to produce something that inevitably draws one away from God is folly. While Solomon was the builder of the temple the text has a deeper meaning: God is the source of our prosperity, our provision, our final product. It is important to recognize in the process of refinement that we allow God to build the house. We do not need to fret, be anxious or worry. We need only to trust God. We rest in the knowledge that He is, in fact, the one that builds the house.

This notion is in direct contradiction to the aforementioned tenant of our culture. Our internal locus of control dictates that we are the ones that control our destiny. This cannot be the mantra of the believer. We are constantly challenged to surrender, to submit our will to God's will, then and only then can we rest.

*Lord God today I choose to rest. I choose to trust You with my circumstances, my well-being, and my life. I will not worry. I will not let fear control my actions. Today and every day I desire to be closer to You. I ask that You continue to draw me closer into Your rest.*

## Day 2

*The LORD is my shepherd, I shall not want. He makes me lie down in green pastures; He leads me beside quiet waters. He restores my soul; He guides me in the paths of righteousness For His name's sake. - Psalm 23:1-3*

Today's scripture is very well known. It is quoted on Christian merchandise; its words have inspired songs and many a Sunday school youth has been cajoled to memorize the passage. Though the words may be very familiar, I would encourage you today to focus on the theme of rest inherent in the passage. Rest is often the first thing that is forgotten in the life of a Christian. We can become so focused on works, good deeds, and doing the right thing that we forgo the rest of the Lord and we cease to rest in the Lord. If the Lord is our shepherd, then like sheep our peace is found in following His plan for our lives. He then can lead us in the paths of righteousness and wholeness. It is only in rest that we can cease from our troubles and our toiling.

Many of us find a false sense of security in our illusion of control. We erroneously believe that we can somehow work hard enough to earn God's favor or blessings. This passage illustrates the folly in that way of thinking. It is only through our total reliance on God that our soul can be restored.

God is willing to be our Shepherd, if we are willing to be His sheep. It is a struggle for some to acknowledge that in our own strength we are insufficient for the task ahead, but it is in this following that we are led to our destiny. Following is at times very counter cultural; we are taught to be strong, independent and self –reliant but the reality is that in most aspects of life we are not independent, but we are interdependent. Today let us relax our control and allow God to lead us in the way we should go.

*Lord, resting for me is uncomfortable. I want to do something. I want to fix something. I want to plan something. Allow me today to rest from my toiling and trust that Your timing is impeccable, and Your plan is perfect.*

## Day 3

*Delight yourself in the Lord;*
*And He will give you the desires of your heart. Commit your way*
*to the Lord, Trust also in Him, and He will do it. He will bring*
*forth your righteousness as the light And your judgment as the*
*noonday.*
*Rest in the Lord and wait patiently for Him... - Psalm 37: 4-7a*

In our times of trouble and conflict, it is easy to forget to trust in God. Christians never really want to admit that we have begun to question the intention of God for our lives. We never truly want to say with our mouths that we think that we could do things in a more efficient, less complex or easy way. Just because we do not admit it does not mean we do not believe it. Unfortunately, when this happens it can cause bitterness in our hearts; we think of all the hardships that we have had to endure and become restless. In these moments, it is imperative that not only are we honest with ourselves but also honest with God.

How can we truly learn to delight ourselves in the Lord without truly exposing ourselves to Him? How can we begin to commit our way to Him and trust Him if we cannot be honest? Honesty and trust are the foundation of rest. One cannot rest if one lacks the feeling of security, in fact, those that walk in restlessness are by definition insecure.

Whatever you seek from refinement the Lord will grant you as you seek after Him, as you commit to Him, as you trust Him. Wherever you are in this moment, you can be assured that God has not left you or led you astray. Rest in the knowledge that God has promised that He will never abandon us or cast us aside. This moment is your moment and as you wait patiently for His plan, He will bring it forth.

*Lord, it is not always easy to wait, it is not always easy to rest. I ask that today You will quiet all the noise, all the distractions, even the chatter of my insecure thoughts. I ask that You bring me a sense of peace, wholeness, and security in You. I ask that You allow me to see beauty in the ever-present essence of Your presence.*

## Day 4

*I wait for the Lord, my soul does wait, And in His word do I hope. My soul waits for the Lord. More than the watchmen for the morning; Indeed, more than the watchmen for the morning. - Psalm 130:5-6*

To understand this passage, it is critical to understand the role of the watchman in ancient societies. In the ancient world, large watchtowers were placed overlooking the fields and storehouses. In the watchtowers, men were appointed to lookout both day and night guarding the fields from animals or from thieves who would make off with the crops ultimately robbing the town of its accumulated resources. Watchtowers were also used as protection from invading armies and other potential threats. As you can imagine there was a great responsibility for the watchmen to be vigilant, on guard and attentive. The watchman was required to stay awake while the town blissfully unaware slumbered. Can you imagine being required to spend all night alone scanning the horizon for some ambiguous ever present but unforeseen threat knowing that if you fail all the families in the town could perish? Now the meaning of the passage becomes clearer. The way that the watchman waits for the break of day, the time of peace, the moment threats have passed and when their duty is absolved, this is the way we wait on the Lord.

The time of waiting on the Lord is an active waiting, it is not merely standing idly by. In essence, it is waiting with bated breath for God to do something. It is waiting with an expectation for God to move with intention and precision. Even during times of rest, we must be aware of God's design and plan for even our resting is purposeful.

*Lord, I wait for You. I wait with expectation. I wait with intention. I wait, knowing that You can move. I wait and, in my waiting, I choose not to trust what I may see with my eyes or feel in my heart, but I trust You God of my salvation. I place all my confidence in the truth that You are with me and even my waiting is designed to give You glory.*

## Day 5

*The Lord reigns forever; He has established His throne for judgment. He rules the world in righteousness and judges the peoples with equity. The Lord is a refuge for the oppressed, a stronghold in times of trouble. Those who know your name trust in you, for you, Lord, have never forsaken those who seek you.*
*Psalm 9:7-10*

Refinement is an ongoing and cyclical process. You are never finished being refined which can be very frustrating for some believers. Humanity seems to have an innate desire to be finished or perfected, but this only occurs when we are reunited with the Father after our physical body ceases to exist. This makes the process of refinement appear unbearable, an impossible and eternal task. We question our own inadequacies, imperfections, and flaws. We want to be fixed and whole quickly and with as little pain as possible. We look in the natural and wonder if God truly is as benevolent as we believe. Why would a righteous and just God allow His people to be oppressed and in a position of struggle? However, we are remiss in our understanding that healing even in the natural is rarely pain free! In times of refining God is still God.

As this scripture notes the Lord is our place of refuge even in these times. He offers a place of safety and rest though this does not always mean our troubles are over or our process complete. We must be reminded that we are required to place our trust in God. Trusting in God is the primary goal of faith. Even when we cannot see the resolution, faith is trusting that a resolution not only exists but is available to us.

When we are weary or pressed beyond our ability to understand it behooves us to call on the name of our God. He has promised never to leave us or abandon us even in the difficult times He remains ever present.

*Lord, I feel like this struggle will never cease. I feel like this season may never end. Give me what I need to see You in every place my feet may tread. Give me peace as You are my refuge and strength. Give me hope that I may see Your glory.*

## Day 6

*My soul, wait in silence for God only, For my hope is from Him. He only is my rock and my salvation, My stronghold; I shall not be shaken. On God, my salvation and my glory rest; The rock of my strength, my refuge is in God. Trust in Him at all times, O people; Pour out your heart before Him; God is a refuge for us. Selah. - Psalm 62:5-12*

Life takes us through many twists and turns. We will see rough times and smooth places. We will face onslaughts and attacks yet there will be times of peace and tranquility. This can produce a roller coaster of emotions for even the most seasoned saint. When one feels jostled it can produce anxiety and panic. Anxiety can be crippling because it causes one to fret about circumstances which cannot be controlled.

If one is not steadily grounded in Christ, this can produce emotional destruction and calamity. The Lord must be your rock and your foundation, otherwise disaster can ensue. We must be mindful that as this journey toward spiritual refinement is one that has multiple stages each with its own challenges and obstacles, only in Christ can we find a secure foundation.

A stronghold can be defined in two ways the first meaning is a place that has been fortified to protect it against attack as in a fortress, fort, castle, citadel or garrison, the second is a place where a particular cause or belief is strongly defended or upheld. In this passage, both meanings are utilized. In

God, we are protected against the attacks of the enemy and at the same time, it is our trust and faith in God that allows us to be unwavering in our commitment to Him. We are reminded that this premise is our focus and our goal. It is not merely enough to be secured by God, but we must also be secure in Him; knowing that above all things He is our refuge and our strength.

*Lord God, You are my refuge and my strength. I put my trust in You. Fellowship with me on the mountain top and walk with me in the valley. Show me your perfect plan for today and every day.*

## Day 7

*The Lord is your keeper; The Lord is your shade on your right hand. The sun will not smite you by day, Nor the moon by night. The Lord will protect you from all evil; He will keep your soul. The Lord will guard your going out and your coming in. From this time forth and forever. - Psalm 121:5-8*

Moving forward in the refinement process can cause unpleasant feelings. There can be a sense of being unsettled and or anxious. There are times when God gives us insight or foreknowing about what things are about to occur. Having only the outline of the plan rather than having full knowledge of what is to come can create fear or foreboding. However, in these moments, it is imperative to remember that God is never going to place you in a position where you are alone. God is ever present in your environment. His plans are meant to progress you, refine and mature you. God is our shade in a hot and thirsty land. God is our moon in the darkness of midnight. The Lord will protect you from evil intent on destroying or harming you. Knowing that God will guard you, not only at this moment but throughout time, through your process and through your journey can help when times of transition occur. During the labor and delivery process the most challenging part is called transition. It is painful and often slow, but it is the precursor to birth. You must go through transition to produce life in both the natural and the spiritual. While that does not mean that transition will be easy, it does mean that changes, advancements, and shifts will be bearable. The Lord will journey with you, He will not leave you. You are His child and the workmanship of His hands.

As the masterpiece that is your life is crafted, be reminded that each twist and turn, each dip in the water is purposeful and, in many ways, intentional. It is all designed to bring you to a place of strength.

*Lord, it is sometimes difficult to trust Your process. There are times when I believe that I can get better results if I would only do things my way. Lord continue to remind me that Your ways are not my ways Your thoughts not my thoughts. Lord allow me to move forward with the knowledge that You will protect me at every turn even from myself.*

Week 4

**Grinding**

At this point in the process of sword crafting, the blacksmith must do the hard work of grinding. While the sword has essentially its final form and shape. it is dull and not fit for its intended use. In order for the shaped metal to achieve its sharp cutting blade, it must be ground. The blacksmith uses various types of grinders to work out the edge and point of the sword. Different types of sword shapes and lengths will need different types of grinding to produce the desired edge. This would also be the point at which any engraving or intricate details would be added to the sword. During this week we will focus on grinding, the part of the Christian walk where God is challenging you to be even more in tune with Him.

Many seasoned saints can get stuck at this stage because after walking for some time with the Lord, there is always a temptation to feel that no further refinement is needed. Like the church of Ephesus, we can become complacent with just the proverbial shape and appearance of being a Christian. We must be mindful that there is further crafting that has yet to occur. Just as in the natural the sword begins this stage with the semblance of a sword, but it lacks the strength or physical properties that will allow the sword to be effective, sharp and usable. This is not a completed sword yet. It is still much too soft.

Popular culture often refers to the "grind" as daily on-going work. It can be repetitive and monotonous. There is always an end goal in mind for such toil. Keeping the focus on God, His purposes, His plans are critical to mastery at this stage.

Day 1

*But if you will seek God earnestly and plead with the Almighty, if you are pure and upright, even now he will rouse himself on your behalf and restore you to your prosperous state. Your beginnings will seem humble, so prosperous will your future be.*
*- Job 8:5-7*

There are times in life when our perceptions are distorted. When we have tough times or hard days, we seek to find the meaning of our discomfort. Generally, we assume that we must be "doing something wrong or not being good enough". During this time, we look at our lives compared to others. We erroneously assess ourselves with a rubric that was never meant for us. We see their successes, triumphs, we see their progression and elevation; we begin to question the path God has set us on. This thought is not foreign. I would suppose that every believer has had a "grass is greener experience" (we know David did). However, note in the text "even now" God is working on your behalf. No matter where you are in your situation God has the ability and desire to use it to prosper you and not to harm you. It is God's desire that your latter days be better than those in the past and even in the present, therefore there is nothing but futility in comparing oneself to others. These types of comparisons are as ridiculous as trying to drink broth with a spoon! The only benchmark you must reach is tailor made for you. There is no competition because you are running your own race in a lane all by yourself. The only qualifying factor is that you run as hard as you can after God by seeking Him earnestly with the entirety of your heart.

Your story is your story. Though your beginning may seem humble or modest ,it is not a predictor of how great your future is destined to be. Remember not to be dismayed for God is bringing you to a most prosperous place.

*Lord God, I ask that today You would help me to see clearly. I ask that you allow me to see all the things that are useful. Lord shield me from thoughts, opinions, and emotions that do not line up with Your will for my life.*

## Day 2

> *But we have this treasure in earthen vessels, so that the surpassing greatness of the power will be of God and not from ourselves; we are afflicted in every way, but not crushed; perplexed, but not despairing; persecuted, but not forsaken; struck down, but not destroyed; always carrying about in the body the dying of Jesus, so that the life of Jesus also may be manifested in our body. - 2 Corinthians 4: 7-10*

This passage highlights the importance of remaining humble throughout the process of being crafted. It allows us to see the beauty in being pressed. Before diamonds are formed from coal, coal is dirty and marred like most of us prior to our encounter with Christ. Coal will remain coal if the atmosphere around it remains the same, in other words, if nothing occurs to prompt the metamorphosis the coal will be just as it is, strong and useful but dirty and relatively unattractive. For the coal to become a diamond which is beautiful, strong and illuminating, there must be pressure and heat. Often, we ask God to deliver us from the "pressure" of life. There are times when we think, "Lord, I have gone through enough, I just want to get out of this place and be free of this pressure!" However, God knows just the right amount of "pressure" that will produce brilliance in us. He knows as only a loving Father can know much we can take and how much refinement we need to become refractors and reflectors of His light. Oftentimes it takes the "pressure" of God to not only force out the impurities, but show us just how strong we are, how resilient we are and ultimately it is this process, that produces the type of light, shimmering and glimmering that draws other people to Christ. Yes, it is uncomfortable and there are times that we would rather not go through the process but without it, the great destiny that God has planned for us, can be derailed, delayed or deferred.

*Lord, I pray that we come to see the value of the "pressure" and look forward to the result regardless of how we feel in the midst of it. Your plan for our lives is the absolute best plan possible beyond what we could ask or think.*

## Day 3

*Truly, truly, I say to you, unless a grain of wheat falls into the earth and dies, it remains alone; but if it dies, it bears much fruit. He who loves his life loses it, and he who hates his life in this world will keep it to life eternal. - John 24:12*

Throughout the life of the believer, there are often sudden seemingly unforeseen changes. These can be jolting and scary. In a recent moment the Lord reminded me of John 12:24. In order to bring forth fruit, there are things in us that must die. Just like the seed must cease to be a seed if it is to reach its full potential as a plant, we too must allow certain attributes or qualities to die to move forward in God. Dying can be painful, unexpected and devastating. God often requires elements of ourselves that are dear to us mindsets, habits, relationships, and ministries which at one time were a part of our identity. But the moment we have grown out of them no matter how prosperous or how comfortable they once were, they must be put to rest. We cannot receive God new things if our hands are still filled with the old things. Old does not mean bad rather it signifies something that is outdated and no longer useful in this context.

Many of us are holding on to the "seed" stage when God is pushing us into the sproutling stage. God is calling us forward, but we remain anchored to the past. If we cling to what we know, if we refuse to change, then we never progress, we never move from seed to sproutling, to sapling, to fruit bearing. We become stagnant and no longer profitable, we are useless and unable to illustrate God's power in our lives. We must not allow fear of mourning the stage that we are in, to force us to forgo the stage that God is calling us to enter. Today be determined to move forward in God's plan for you, no matter what and if it feels like you are dying, celebrate you are doing something right!

*Lord God let this season in my life bare abundant fruit. Though the process of baring fruit requires weeding and pruning, I ask that You do what You will to cause my fruit to flourish in the spiritual realm. Your plans for me are perfect so even if it hurts, I will trust You.*

## Day 4

*Samuel said, "Has the Lord as much delight in burnt offerings and sacrifices As in obeying the voice of the Lord? Behold, to obey is better than sacrifice,*
*And to heed than the fat of rams. - Samuel 15:22*

Have you ever heard the common saying "Obedience is better than sacrifice?" Unlike some common misrepresentations such as, "God only helps those who help themselves", the former is found in the biblical text. Perhaps the reason obedience is better than sacrifice is that true obedience is a sacrifice. We all know that if someone asks us to do something we want to do, it is effortless and we do it with no problem. We don't have to pray about it, we don't have to ponder the cost benefit ratio and we often do not look for a reciprocal response. However, when someone (especially a higher authority) TELLS us to do something we don't want to do, we have a huge issue with that! We make snide remarks, get an attitude or become passive aggressive toward the individual. Why do we do this? I believe the cause is the sinful nature of humanity. Without parameters and refinement, people can be hedonistic at the core; we want to do only what we want to do, when we like and how we prefer to perform the task. When God asks us to obey Him, it forces us to give up the part of ourselves that gets to make our self-absorbed decisions; the part of us that we often refer to as the flesh is buffeted by such obedience. Often when we are obedient to God we are not gratifying our own desires, rather we are forsaking our plans for God's divine will. Obedience is a sacrifice, but I promise you the sacrifice is worth it!

*Father, I admit that there are times when I desire to do it my way. I know that my way is most often not the best way but it is the way my will takes me. Lord thank You for the times Your grace and mercy has covered my stubbornness or self-centered actions. I ask that You continue to teach me that obedience is better than sacrifice.*

## Day 5

*He who loves his life will lose it, and he who hates his life in this world will keep it for eternal life. If anyone serves Me, let him follow Me; and where I am, there My servant will be also. If anyone serves Me, him My Father will honor. - John 12:25-26*

Grinding something takes away parts of the whole. Imagine a grindstone; a thick disk of stone or other abrasive material is made to revolve so that other objects can be ground against it. A grindstone is used for grinding, sharpening, or polishing metal objects. As the metal is scraped across the harsh abrasive material small particles are sloughed off in efforts to improve the sharpness and acuity of the blade. This happens in our spiritual life as well. There are moments where we are locked in the grinding period. During this season we may be tempted to forget that the life of the Christian is not one of perpetual roses or lollipops. Christianity requires sacrifice on a level which allows portions of self to be scraped away. Rarely does this happen gently, like Paul on the road to Damascus we must be jolted into renewal and restoration. We must be both retooled and repurposed when we desire to be used by God. This will cause us to lose elements that are no longer able to produce God's intended or desired effect. This can be confusing, painful and cause distress because we are required to let go of ourselves now in favor of the new creature we are becoming. The harsh reality is that this is what must occur if we want to truly live, if we want to walk in the newness of Christ, and if we want to die to the flesh. This process is crucial to our spiritual sharpness and it is one that continues as we grow in God. The more sharpened we are, the more fully we can be used by God which ultimately brings glory and honor to Him.

*Merciful and loving Father, I know that Your process of refinement is designed for my good. I believe that everything I may lose, though painful, is going to be the best for me. Even when I cannot see the end from the beginning, I know that you will sustain me. I will be used for your glory!*

## Day 6

> *"Do not be afraid," Samuel replied. "You have done all this evil; yet do not turn away from the Lord, but serve the Lord with all your heart. Do not turn away after useless idols. They can do you no good, nor can they rescue you, because they are useless. For the sake of his great name the Lord will not reject his people, because the Lord was pleased to make you his own. - 1 Samuel 12:20-22*

During refinement there are times when we in our frailty might deliberately choose to do the wrong thing. The passage discusses the nation of Israel and their rejection of God, their idol worship, and desire for a king. We can say how evil Israel is for this series of offenses against God or we can commiserate and empathize. We too have fallen short of the expectations of God. It is a crucial act of refinement to be able to examine shortcomings. Without being honest and transparent, no change can be wrought. It is often when a Christian commits a sin or becomes trapped in a pattern of sin that they turn their face from God. Like Adam in the garden, it can be instinctual to hide after an individual has committed an act that deliberately goes against God. Hiding is the exact opposite of what we should do. Acknowledging that sin has occurred and accepting responsibility for the part that we played in committing the act is the first part of moving forward. The acknowledgement of sin is not the only part we are required to play rather it is the first step in the process. The next step is equally important. You must decide to no longer engage in the offensive behavior so that deliberate purposeful change is born. While it is easier said than done, rerouting your natural thoughts and inclinations becomes easier over time. When you spend intentional time with God in prayer, mediation, study and fasting it becomes easier to resist the temptation of the enemy.

*Lord, thank You for reminding me that though I fail, though I am far from perfect, Your grace extends beyond my ability to mess things up! Thank you for reminding me that You know about every error and You love me just the same. I ask that as I turn from my sin to honor You, You will continue to make sin less attractive.*

## Day 7

*For I am convinced that neither death, nor life, nor angels, nor principalities, nor things present, nor things to come, nor powers, nor height, nor depth, nor any other created thing, will be able to separate us from the love of God, which is in Christ Jesus our Lord. - Romans 8:37-39*

During the grinding process it may feel overwhelming, crushing and impossible to understand. This can happen because we are not always able to recognize refinement in the moment which it is occurring. When things in your life become more difficult be reminded that God's hand is still with you. While God is not the author of evil, there are times when He allows it in His infinite wisdom. This can be a very difficult concept to accept. We think of horrific tragedies; horrible acts of violence and insidious diseases, and question God's design. I implore you in this moment to run hastily to the arms of God rather than turning away. God can bear your feelings and emotions. He is not offended when you are honest with Him. Like with Job, He may just be silent, or you may be granted with a response. There is nothing that can separate God's children from the Father, the scripture gives a list of circumstances; however it is far from exhaustive, therefore the use of the word nothing covers all circumstances. There is nothing!!!!! That can separate us from God's love for those that believe! The most important thing is to remember that in all these things you are not walking alone, God is with you. Though you are going through various tests, trials, tribulation, and heartbreak, God is there through every agonizing moment! He will as He promised use it for your good whether in this life or the next. You will always be victorious. You will win because the God of the universe does not lie, and the God of the universe promised you would.

*It becomes hard to see You when difficult times come. I feel abandoned and forgotten. Lord thank you for every time You show me, I am not alone. Through all the twist and turns, hills and valleys and through every lush garden or arid desert. You will never cast me aside. Thank You for reminding me.*

Week 5

**Hardening**

The sword at this time is fully recognizable as a sword; its shape is fixed and its blade sharpened. It is not however complete, the metal while stable is soft and prone to breaking. It is now time for the intense process of hardening. The almost finished work is heated to a very high temperature and then placed into a quenching tank. This quenching allows it to cool quickly and evenly which will harden the metal.

In our process of spiritual refinement, this is the time where God allows the additional work which will solidify and anchor our thinking later. The hardening process is different for everyone and may look different in various lives. For most people it is a time where the proverbial fire is turned up; however, the peace and wisdom of God are present in such a way that the individual, though challenged, is not destroyed. It is during this phase that a greater intimacy with God is cultivated and nurtured. This is when praise and worship are no longer something that you do rather something that you are, your life and lifestyle become a fragrant worship to God. This foundation of trust, rest and total reliance on God propels you even closer to Him and His will for your life.

This stage is one that requires wisdom, dedication, and intention. One is not haphazardly hardened, but one is crafted to be hardened and, in many ways, one must continue to endure temptation, trails, and circumstances on a new level. At the onset of this time one may feel frustrated and agitated as circumstances come to buffet and challenge you. It is imperative in these moments that you can identify this season of intentionally relying on God is critical to your later ability to hear from and rest in His will by His grace.

## Day 1

*Let your eyes look directly ahead and let your gaze be fixed straight in front of you. Watch the path of your feet And all your ways will be established. Do not turn to the right nor to the left; Turn your foot from evil. - Proverbs 4:25-27*

Throughout the challenges of life, one may be tempted to take his eyes not only off the One who sets the path, but also off the path itself. There are many illustrations in the biblical text that show how men and women of God, who were once emblazoned with desire for God's will suddenly become complacent or unmotivated. Like Moses, it may be due to disappointment or frustrations with others. Perhaps, like Job it may be due to life circumstances and personal troubles. No matter the cause, it is imperative to remember to keep your eyes straight ahead. Looking solely at what is around you will only serve as an invitation to self-doubt, fear, confusion and ultimately anger towards God.

This is not to say that you will not have moments of wavering, rather if you are sidetracked for any reason or any length of time ,know that the solution is always to return you gaze to the loving image of our Father.

This is what it means to journey with God, He is the One whom we follow. Our trust, our security, and our convictions are found in Him. This is the only way that the cares of this life will not encumber or overtake us. Refocusing on God is not difficult or laborious, we must simply learn how to spend intimate dedicated time with the Lord. When we look to God, even in our confusion or discomfort, He is there to gently encourage, nudge or reassure us in the direction that He has designed for us. Lastly if we do fall, we are assured that He will be there to help us up.

*Lord, help me to keep my eyes fixed on Your plan for my life. Lord, anchor my heart in Your will and Your plan. Help me to discern evil and those things that would ensnare me, always allow my hand to be secured with Your hand always.*

## Day 2

*The spirit of a man can endure his sickness, but as for a broken spirit who can bear it? The mind of the prudent acquires knowledge, and the ear of the wise seeks knowledge. A man's gift makes room for him and brings him before great men. - Proverbs 18:14-16*

Today's scripture prompts us to recall that it is very important to be mindful of how you think. The way one processes and compartmentalizes information can be a springboard to future success or failure. Having to endure hardships or difficult times can cause a person to feel heavy, overburdened and downtrodden. While we know cognitively that challenges and circumstances will come to test our mettle and our faith, this does not mean that it is easy to go through the circumstances. Finding ways to thrive even in an adverse environment is an important part of spiritual refinement.

Examining what is happening not only around you but inside of you by processing one's internal dialogue and rationale, helps us to have a level of self-knowledge and understanding. Focusing on the positive rather than dwelling on the negative can motivate, push, and propel you forward to your destiny. But focusing on negativity in any form can hinder you.

Acquiring knowledge in the context of this scripture is more than an earthly or academic knowledge; it is seeking the face of God for meaning, purpose and true understanding of the matters of life. When you do this, your gifts and talents make room for you. Your life and light then draw others to you in a way that ultimately brings glory to your heavenly Father.

*Lord God help me today to see You in all things! Let me see You in my good times, my difficult times and my times of questioning. Lord, grant me wisdom and knowledge to travel through this process. Lord cast out my doubting and fear and remind me of my refinement, my purpose, and Your plan.*

## Day 3

*The plans of the heart belong to man,*
*But the answer of the tongue is from the Lord.*
*All the ways of a man are clean in his own sight,*
*But the Lord weighs the motives. Commit your works to the Lord*
*And your plans will be established. - Proverbs 16:1-3*

There are often moments during the process of refinement where we believe that we have a more efficient plan than the one prepared by God. We do this with partial obedience to the things that God is asking us to do. The scripture warns that there is great danger in this! Our human finite minds are not able to craft a better plan than our Heavenly Father. We may think we know better but really, our vision and our planning will always come up short. We have hidden thoughts and secret motives. We operate from the pain of our past and the fear of our futures. While we weigh only what we can discern in our limited ability, insight and understanding, God weighs everything throughout all eternity with His wisdom and expertise. There is no result or consequence that escapes Him at any time. Therefore, it is exceedingly wise to place all our plans, goals and pursuits before Him. Each aspect of our lives should be submitted to the Lord of our lives.

We do this through the practice of spiritual disciplines. Prayer, fasting and spending intentional time meditating on the word of God leads to the clarity of His will for us individually and collectively. In this way we take the risk and the guesswork out of our endeavors to have the guarantee that it will work out in the end for our good. When you commit your works to the Lord, you honor him with your life, you honor Him with your obedience, you honor Him with your plans.

*Lord God, I know your plans for me are good. I know Your plans for me are without flaw. Help me to submit to Your will trusting and acknowledging that You have my very best interest at heart. Knowing that You are using every experience, test, and triumph to produce something meaningful and beneficial in my life.*

## Day 4

*Do not love sleep or you will grow poor; stay awake and you will have food to spare. "It's no good, it's no good!" says the buyer—then goes off and boasts about the purchase. Gold there is, and rubies in abundance, but lips that speak knowledge are a rare jewel. - Proverbs 20:13-16*

There are several concepts in today's reading, the first is that a person must put plans into motion. It is not enough to have ideas, aspirations or inspiration, rather it is crucial to be motivated to manifest. In this spiritual journey, one must take account of this concept not only when it comes to making money but in any form of production. It is our task to refine, replicate and reproduce. The good that we discover by being in relationship with the Lord should be spread to others. This spreading takes clear, concerted and intentional action.

The second concept has to do with acknowledging when an error has occurred. During our journey, there are times when we may make the wrong choice or, in our human frailty, act in a way that displeases God. This is a natural condition of the fallen state of man. Intermittent failure or shortcomings are to be expected, but the folly occurs when we refuse to acknowledge them or hold ourselves accountable. It is imperative that we accept our errors to move forward.

The third concept is that there is an abundance of information, many schools of thought, much advice and outside opinions especially in the modern age but there is a difference between facts and knowledge. Facts are about what you know but knowledge denotes how knowledge is applied. Learning how to translate what you know into something that is useful and helpful to others is infinitely more valuable than just retaining information.

*Lord show me how to utilize all that You have provided me with to be able to move closer to you. Let me be motivated not to be lazy or slothful. Lord, let me acknowledge my sin and move beyond it. Lord, help me not to make the same mistake twice. Lord teach me Your knowledge that surpasses human understanding.*

## Day 5

*One who is gracious to a poor man lends to the LORD, And He will repay him for his good deed. - Proverbs 19:17*

The concept of sowing and reaping is not only a natural law but a theological principle. This is noted multiple times in scripture. The same sentiment is echoed in Luke 6:38 "Give, and it will be given to you. A good measure, pressed down, shaken together, and running over will be poured into your lap. For with the measure you use, it will be measured back to you."

What you plant will take root and grow in some form or fashion. This happens without discrimination or intention. While it is not as arbitrary or indiscriminate as some would like to believe, we do not always get what we expect. Many times, in our journey we have given above and beyond to a cause, a person ,or a vision and seemingly get very little in return on our investment. Does this invalidate this spiritual principle? No, rather it speaks to the heart of our verse today. God is the One that is responsible for payment of good deeds! God is the one who can measure the gift's true value, but God also measures the heart of the person giving the gift. Though we may not see it at first glance, we have in fact received a measure for our efforts, we have grown in faith, we have the fruit of dedication and resilience, and we have a tenacity to press forward when we did not possess that before! God is the Divine Balancer of the checkbook He is the Fiduciary that will never cheat us. We often require God's wisdom to see past the natural things to the spiritual things whether in natural finances or in spiritual currency.

*Help me Father to see the world as you see it. Help me to look beyond the simple math, the list of checks and balances that I keep in my head. Help me to see the needs of others past my own comfort. Lord allow me to love my brother and sisters even more then I love myself, that I can then illustrate to the world how much love You have given Your children.*

## Day 6

*The naive believes everything, But the sensible man considers his steps. A wise man is cautious and turns away from evil, But a fool is arrogant and careless. The naive inherit foolishness, But the sensible are crowned with knowledge. - Proverbs 14:15-16, 18*

As one goes through life it is vital to understand the difference between being intelligent and walking in wisdom. The ability to retain information is often how we judge a person's intellectual ability. We look at test scores and I.Q numbers, but all the intelligence in the world is no match for the wisdom of God. Wisdom is the opposite of naivety and it only can be acquired through the gift of God. Wisdom is the ability to translate knowledge into something usable, something that can be practically applied. Wisdom allows a person to be cautious and discerning in both natural and spiritual things. Those with intelligence can be pompous and arrogant. Our scripture warns against this as arrogance limits one's ability to see the whole picture. Arrogance is foolish because it assumes that one individual has some greater value than another person. In the economy of God, this is never the case. Wisdom is something that affects not only the person who has it, but also can help others avoid calamity. We have all been the recipient of a wise word given to us by someone else. I can only be used in this capacity if I am humble and kind, after all, who listens to people that walk-in pompousness and arrogance? We must be mindful that the sensible are crowned with knowledge, in contrast the naïve inherit foolishness. To avoid folly, we must first spend time with God. God is the source of true wisdom sitting at His feet is the only way to perfect the spiritual gifts afforded to us when we receive salvation. To omit this portion of our journey is truly foolish.

*Lord grant me with Your wisdom and teach me how to apply it, share it and multiply it.*
*Lord help me to acquire wisdom to utilize the knowledge that You have graced me with. Lord use me to help others grasp spiritual concepts.*

## Day 7

*Get wisdom, get understanding: forget it not; neither decline from the words of my mouth. Forsake her not, and she shall preserve thee: love her, and she shall keep thee. Wisdom is the principal thing; therefore, get wisdom: and with all thy getting get understanding. - Proverbs 4:5-7*

Being refined is not a task that is to be taken lightly in either the spiritual or the natural realm. It requires strength and endurance of the craftsman. It requires enduring high temperatures, uncomfortable environments and hot metal. It requires the material to be manipulated from ore to a stunning work that is ready to be used. In the example of a sword, lives depend on whether the work was done well and correctly. During this process, it is important to remember that what is happening inside of you is not only for you but also for others. The hardening occurs in such a way that you gain wisdom but also are intentional about making it a part of your life. You learn in order to increase knowledge, wisdom, and understanding. Your task as you move toward the next stage to learn how to apply the wisdom of God to your life and the lives of those connected to you. Do not forsake the wisdom of God, life outside of the will of God is reminiscent of an empty shell or an outline to a great story with none of the content. There is something fulfilling and gratifying about operating in your God crafted assignment.

There is some security and trust when you know without a shadow of a doubt that you are indeed doing what the Lord would have you to do.

Wisdom is a requirement for the Spirit led life. It is wisdom that keeps us from sins of omission and sins of commission. We not only know that right thing to do but we also know the consequences of not doing what we should.

*Lord thank You for granting me wisdom that surpasses my own. Thank You for not hiding your face from me. Thank You for allowing me the strength to endure the journey. Lord that You for allowing me to understand even as I go to the next level in You.*

## Week 6

## Tempering

During the process of tempering the blade is heated and quenched once again. While this process is like hardening now the heating is at a much lower temperature. This can be viewed as much less intense than in previous stages. This heating/quenching cycle may be repeated several times. This tempering allows the blade to be strong but not brittle. It will have a certain amount of flexibility yet still retain its sharp edge.

It is important for Christians to be both strong and flexible. As agents of Christ in the world, we should be mindful that we are connected to other people. Learning how to live the principles of God and apply them to our lives is important in our process of spiritual refinement. Building relationships in the body of Christ is equated to this tempering process. God made us be social, emotional beings; therefore, being in a relationship with others is not inherently difficult. However, if you are one that has been hurt repeatedly by others it can feel like a very arduous task to risk getting hurt again.

Tempering in the process of refinement is not an event but a process. Time and intention are required to build strength that will not buckle under pressure yet flexibility which adjust to the occasion.

Repetition occurs to create something that is both strong but also has the capacity to bend not break. The following week will focus on forgiveness and relationships as this is one of the final steps of refinement: transitioning from being introspective to having a relational interdependent outlook. God desires us to love Him and love each other without exception. In order to be used effectively by the Lord one must be aligned with His capacity to love without fail and to forgive at a moment's notice in the face of offense?

## Day 1

*Beloved, let us love one another, for love is from God; and everyone who loves is born of God and knows God. The one who does not love does not know God, for God is love. - 1 John 4:7-8*

One of the hallmarks of refinement is how we interact with one another. The scripture implies that as we are loved by God there is a mandate on our lives to share that very same love with others. If God is love, those that are His children are required to love. It is not optional or up for debate. The scripture is very clear and there is no ambiguity. Christians do not have the option to hate, discard or ostracize others. Being born of God means that Christians have a responsibility to conduct themselves in a way that pleases the Father just as the behavior of one's children is often used as a way to evaluate the diligence and example of the parents. Our behavior reflects positively or negatively on God.

While it may appear to be convenient in this capitalistic world to look at people for only what they can produce, this is not God's way. God looks at His children with eyes of love, contentment and hope. It is therefore our job to look at this world with those very same eyes.

It is God's desire to now use us to reach people in their unfinished and unrefined state. When we see people, who are proverbially "rough around the edges", we are not to flee. We are now in a position to see individuals in the refinement process and love them through their journey, through their forging and grinding. We are commissioned to do this not because it is easy rather because it is necessary. We do this because in journeying with others we partake in our own perpetual refinement it is through this process that we are sharpened even more.

*Lord thank You for privileging me to love. Loving other is not always easy. Though I struggle with my ability to see You, in all people and at all times. Please show me to love past my limitations. Teach me to love as You do.*

## Day 2

*Be completely humble and gentle; be patient, bearing with one another in love. Make every effort to keep the unity of the Spirit through the bond of peace. There is one body and one Spirit, just as you were called to one hope when you were called; one Lord, one faith, one baptism; one God and Father of all, who is over all and through all and in all. - Ephesians 4:2-6*

One of the most challenging tasks in our journey is learning how to be humble and gentle. In many cases, our environments and our past encounters have produced a faint aroma of skepticism, cynicism, and caution. Many individuals travel through life with a very hard emotional exterior meant to protect them from all things that could potentially hurt us, especially other people. Though we may protect our fragile hearts from betrayal and disappointment, we also limit our own capacity to love others. Like armor designed to protect the knights of antiquity, while there is protection, there is also limited range of motion and emotion. It is hard to walk in unity with others when you have been hurt, rejected or rebuffed. It is twice as hard to walk in this world isolated, alone and inaccessible to others.

We are to make every effort to keep the unity of peace between our brothers and sisters in Christ; we cannot use the excuse of being hurt as an exemption to following the command of Christ. Loving one another and using our collective gifts in the corporate body of Christ is not negotiable or optional; it is a mandatory part of being the church.

We were called into the family of God, we acknowledge that there is one Lord, one faith, one baptism. We have an intimacy not only with God but also with one another illustrating His love for all.

*You know all things, Lord, You know that I have been hurt by people who were Your children. Though they hurt me I ask that You help me open myself to others and love again. By doing this, there is an opportunity that I will be hurt again but there is a greater opportunity to please You.*

## Day 3

*Therefore, as God's chosen people, holy and dearly loved, clothe yourselves with compassion, kindness, humility, gentleness and patience. Bear with each other and forgive one another if any of you has a grievance against someone. Forgive as the Lord forgave you. - Colossians 3:12-13*

Forgiveness is not a foreign concept. People talk about forgiveness a lot, ad nauseam until the word becomes trite and without real meaning. I believe that this is because most people are aware that forgiveness is vital to emotional and spiritual health however, many people struggle, not with saying they forgive, but with truly forgiving. It is customary, common and polite to say, "Yes, I forgive you." all the while holding unforgiveness in the heart. We rehearse the wrongs that people have done to us and then use it to justify our behavior. However, this misses the point of forgiveness in the first place. To forgive means to cancel the debate as if it were never owed. This means that it is as if it never happened! The scale is balanced, there are no further opportunities to collect because the debt is canceled. This is not easy when offenses and transgressions are great, wounds are deep, and consequences from actions may still be present, but forgiveness is more for the offended then the offender.

As one who has been forgiven, it is imperative to remember that forgiveness is at the core of the relationship with God. One cannot walk around holding others accountable for a multitude of sins when they have been forgiven of their own. This is the cry of God's heart which we see repeatedly in the scripture. Forgive, forgive and then forgive again to bring glory and honor to our God.

*Lord, today and everyday help me to move beyond unforgiveness. Heal the wounds of my failed relationships, be the source of my strength when memories of betrayal return, Lord show me how you have always been there with me when I have been battered and bruised. Lord give me the peace that passes my own comprehension.*

## Day 4

*Above all, keep fervent in your love for one another, because love covers a multitude of sins. Be hospitable to one another without complaint. As each one has received a special gift, employ it in serving one another as good stewards of the manifold grace of God. - 1 Peter 4:8-10*

When you think about the expanse of your life it is common to examine the areas where you have fallen victim to another person. At times it is much easier to look at the things that have happened to me rather than to take a spiritual inventory of how our own misdeeds have impacted others. The purpose of being mindful of our past transgressions is not so that we become paralyzed or feel guilty; instead it puts into perspective the things that others may have done to us. When we recognize that we have sinned, first against God, then against each other, we can begin to understand how love covers a multitude of sins.

The people with the most potential to hurt me are the ones that are in the closest proximity to me therefore it is not only improbable but virtually impossible to be in a relationship with another person without hurting them. Yet, because God has created us to be social emotional beings, we do not get a free pass to shut down, isolate or disconnect from others.

Because God has gifted us with love, grace and mercy it is our duty and obligation to extend that same gift to others.

Understanding that love covered a multitude of our sins and now our love can cover a multitude of others. Love has a way of multiplying and increasing, even if it starts small. It is like a little yeast leavening a whole mass of dough or a tiny spark creating a massive fire it only takes one intentional act of love to reconcile.

*Lord let me be mindful of how much love, grace and mercy has been showered upon me. Let me never forget the weight of Your sacrifice. Do not allow me to remain stuck in pain from the wounds of others but show me how love covers a multitude of transgressions.*

## Day 5

> *"The Lord did not set His love on you nor choose you because you were more in number than any of the peoples, for you were the fewest of all peoples, but because the Lord loved you ... Know therefore that the Lord your God, He is God, the faithful God, who keeps His covenant and His lovingkindness to a thousandth generation with those who love Him and keep His commandments. - Deuteronomy 7:7-8a,9*

Knowing that God has chosen to love us even with all our imperfections and flaws helps us to understand the criteria for love. We see that love is not something that can be earned, rather it is an active choice. Love does not occur haphazardly. rather it requires intentional effort. Love requires tenacity and perseverance. Love requires a faithfulness that does not wax and wane. Love keeps its promises and fulfills its obligations.

This standard is high; however, it is the standard that has been set before us by our Heavenly Father. We are to focus and press to copy the pattern of love that we have been shown. We must fix our minds to strive toward the love principle. The outline has been given to us plainly and clearly in our own experience.

The Lord has loved us from our preconception until now, before we could do anything to earn His love, before any gifts or talents, before potential could be seen. It is with knowledge that we purpose in our hearts to operate in love. God's own design is for His children to reflect and replicate His love. This is the key to living a life of purpose and fulfillment. God is faithful to us and illustrates his lavish love on us daily when you feel unable to love and to reflect on the times when He has poured His love onto you without you being able to earn it. True love is a gift, a gift cannot be earned. The moment one is required to earn a gift, it ceases to be a gift and becomes a reward.

*Lord let me be reminded that I am yours. You are faithful You are just, You are loving and kind . Lord remind me of how much You have delighted in having a relationship with me. Let me have that same zeal for others.*

## Day 6

*The weapons we fight with are not the weapons of the world. On the contrary, they have divine power to demolish strongholds. We demolish arguments and every pretension that sets itself up against the knowledge of God, and we take captive every thought to make it obedient to Christ. - 2 Cor. 10:4-5*

When considering love and forgiveness we must also consider that our pain in relationships begins in our own mind and heart. There are times when transgressions which occurred that are seemingly very small have injured us severely. This happens because we carry the pain of previous heartbreak, rejection and or disappointment. The result is that we then walk around with a perpetual fear of being hurt. Fear exists because we ruminate on all the negative possibilities of what has happened and what could happen instead of focusing on the moment we are experiencing right now. We know in our mind what we should do to be loving, kind and forgiving but the fear in our hearts prevents us from doing so.

This is a tool that the enemy uses to keep us immovable and stagnated. If we operate in fear and trepidation, we will advance and grow at a slower rate. Fear has the capacity to hinder every life changing decision and makes it difficult to pursue God's perfect plan for our lives. Perhaps most importantly perfect love casts out fear therefore, love and fear cannot dwell in the same place. Love is reckless in its pursuit of us, we must be equally tenacious in perusing it. We must intend to demolish every thought that is contrary to God's love for us and God's mandate to love others.

*Lord, purify my mind. Keep my mind in perfect peace. Help me live in the gift of today rather than the pain of the past or the anxiety of the future. Help me to see Your will for my life and my relationships.*

## Day 7

*Beloved, let us love one another, for love is from God; and everyone who loves is born of God and knows God. The one who does not love does not know God, for God is love.* - 1 John 4:7-8

You will notice that this passage has been used previously at the beginning of the week. I believe that God can speak to us in a multitude of ways and often using the same text. We have already discussed how imperative it is to love one another; however we did not highlight how much this is essential to the Christian faith. This passage indicates that those who do not love, do not know God, because God is love. This means that knowing God is synonymous with knowing love. This does not mean that one automatically knows how to put the principle of love into practice, rather it denotes that at least one has encountered the illustration of love. Simply put it is impossible to love purely without having first experiencing an illustration of love. Because love is not merely a feeling, rather a conscious active choice, it has a methodology that must be emulated and learned rather than merely manufactured based on feelings and emotions. Knowing God gives us the blueprint on how to love by experiencing the all-encompassing, self-sacrificing love of God. This illustrates not only how to reciprocate His

Love for us but also how to love ourselves and others. Christians that "know" God but are mean, cantankerous and difficult know of but have not yet received revelation of God's love. Being aware of God's love but not embracing it often produces a skewed perception of love and forgiveness. As you truly understand the sacrifice which occurred to demonstrate God's love for us, you become transformed.

*Lord God that You for Your illustration of love. Thank You for loving me when I have not loved You with my whole heart. Thank You for empowering me to love. Today, I choose to love.*

Week 7

**Completion**

The sword blade itself is now complete. The artisan has completed His work, and this is the time when the work is embellished. Engraving occurs, adornments are added, and all the final touches are added. In the spiritual journey, the completion stage cannot be confined to this lifetime because we are constantly being refined and crafted. Therefore, this week will consist of guided reflections to help evaluate your position in the forge. This concluding week is designed to be used with intention along with dedicated time to fellowship with God.

Carve out a time each day when you can be undisturbed for at least thirty minutes. Grab a pen and extra paper to record any insights you may uncover. Open your heart earnestly to listen to what the Lord is saying to you as you answer the questions. Take the time to reflect on your journey over the past few weeks and be mindful of any elements that can be taken with you as you continue your journey. If you are able, I would encourage you to set your mind to fast this week to buffet your body and focus your attention on God and what God is saying to you.

Know that God will speak as you listen to His voice. Acknowledge His presence in your time of reflection and listen intently with expectation.

## Day 1

### What kind of metal?

What are some qualities that I have which are valuable or useful to God?

_____
_____
_____
_____

In what type of environment do I excel?

_____
_____
_____
_____

Are there any areas in my life where I feel out of place or disjointed?

_____
_____
_____
_____

Am I walking in the direction of God's plan?

Have there been times when I have told myself that I am not valuable?




I define myself as...




Who does God say I am?

What is the Lord saying to you right now?

___

*Lord, I thank You for choosing me. Thank you for reminding me of who I am and how I can be used by You. Thank You for expanding my perceptions of myself.*

## Day 2

### The Forge

When adversity occurs, what scriptures come to mind?

___

How has God used difficult times to highlight your character?

___

What are some areas in your life that you know need to be relinquished, refined, or refurbished?

___

What feelings are most present for you today?

How can you use your present spiritual process to help others?

How is pain beneficial to your growth and development?

How have you been hindered in your refinement process and how can you now begin to move forward?

_____
_____
_____
_____
_____
_____
_____
_____
_____
_____
_____
_____

*Lord thank You for knowing me beyond what I know of myself. Help me to move past my view of myself. Help me to see myself the way that You see me. Help me to withstand the heat of Your forge, to shine with Your brilliance.*

Day 3

**Annealing**

When do you hear the voice of the Lord most profoundly?

Which spiritual disciplines do you find most attractive?

Do you have dedicated or reserved time with the Lord? If so, how do you protect it?

How do you plan to incorporate rest into your dedicated time with the Lord?

When do you feel restless?

What do you do when you feel anxious, overwhelmed, or worried?

How does God's love cast out fear and anxiety?

_____
_____
_____
_____
_____
_____

How can rest help you grow or move forward?

_____
_____
_____
_____
_____
_____
_____
_____
_____
_____
_____
_____

*Lord in the busyness of life Help me to just be!*

Day 4

## Grinding

What are your rough or growing edges?

_____
_____
_____
_____
_____

What character traits do you wrestle with that do not bring glory to God?

_____
_____
_____
_____
_____

What area of your life can be further submitted to the will of God?

_____
_____
_____
_____
_____

What are you afraid of feeling, experiencing or facing in the process of refinement?

How is trust related to yielding to the will of God?

How do you remind yourself that God's plan is good for you?

Where do you see the most growth happening right now?

How can you be more open to the "grinding" process?

_____
_____
_____
_____
_____

*Lord, thank You for the grinding, the striping and the sharpening! While it may not feel good, it is not only good, it is essential.*

Day 5

## Hardening

In what areas have you experienced the Lord stretching your thinking?

_____
_____
_____
_____

How do you define wisdom?

_____
_____
_____
_____

How do you define knowledge?

_____
_____
_____
_____

How do you see "hardening" in operation in your walk with the Lord ?

_____
_____

How do you identify Godly wisdom?

How do you receive the wisdom of God?

How do you put into practice the wisdom of God?

Are there any foolish practices that you need to discontinue?

_____
_____
_____
_____

*I want to know your ways Lord. Help me to grow in Your wisdom and Your knowledge. Take the limits off and let me see beyond my own vision.*

## Day 6

### **Tempering**

Define forgiveness.

_____
_____
_____
_____

Is unforgiveness holding you back? If so, how can you begin the process of forgiveness?

_____
_____
_____
_____

Where are you being stretched in your relationships?

_____
_____
_____
_____

How can your relationships bring glory and honor to God?

_____
_____
_____
_____

How can you be more open to others and their needs?

_____
_____
_____
_____

How can focusing on others further your refinement?

_____
_____
_____
_____

What is the relationship between loving God and loving others?

_____
_____
_____
_____
_____
_____
_____

*You have created me for relationships with others. I know that You have increased my capacity to love others and to see them how You see them. Continue to show me how to truly love.*

Day 7

**Completion**

How have you grown in the last 7 weeks?

_____
_____
_____
_____

How can you see God further refining you?

_____
_____
_____
_____

How do you plan to further your process?

_____
_____
_____
_____
_____
_____
_____
_____

What is your prayer for today?

## My Prayer

It is my hope and sincere prayer that this work helped to further your refining process. Being mindful that this analogy has its limitations and the process of sword making was simplified for the purposes of illustration. We are continually being refined in God's refinery until we join Him for eternity. Each day that we live and breathe we can get closer to Him!

## Acknowledgments

Thank you first to my Lord and Savior Jesus Christ.

Thank you Kashif Hadley my awesome husband, my secret cheerleader who would say all my best ideas come from him and would be mostly right. Thank you for believing I could and motivating me to completion. Eden, Eli'sha and Emmanuel you make me so proud and you have reminded me to stay focused.

Thank you to my grandmother Rosa L. Downing, you inspire me every day your sacrificial love and unshaken faith has been an example. My father Herbert Downing, my dad, whose love for me is soft spoken and unmatched, who sends me encouraging words and always knows the right thing to say at the right time. To my Aunt and Uncle Daniella D. and Godwin G Guerrero who consistently tell me I can do anything I put my mind to, you both have pushed me my entire life. I am forever grateful. Amber and Amirah Guerrero continue to be the amazing women you are thank you for your encouragement.

Natasha West and Sherry West my family for certain and for sure, thank you for always showing up, thank you for being there standing on the sidelines cheering me on!

Thank you, Rev. Bryan Jackson and Family who have been instrumental in my spiritual development and have encouraged me to use my gifts and talents for the Kingdom of God.

To Yolanda Kennard and TiAiria Neal who were relentless in their persistence that I begin writing, who were certain that I had something to share with the people of God, may God bless you for all that you have done for me.

To Danielle J. Mitchell who has listened to many doubts, fears and concerns and told me "So what! Do it anyway." Thank you for giving of yourself and for not letting me squander what the Lord has declared me to write.

To Kanitra Alston, Valerie Garfield, Pastor Charles Brokenborough and Dr. Holly Sawyer who have offered their time, talent and treasure in various measures to see this work come into fruition, I praise God for His work in your lives and thank you so much for being a blessing.
Joaneah Williams and Ashely Smith thank you for bringing my ideas to life in your creative design and artwork. You both are gifted artisans.
Thank you, Paulette Brokenborough and Gwendolyn Baggett, for punctuating me, grammar is not my strong suit!
Thank you, Bishop Michael and Pastor Denise Brokenborough, for your leadership and support. Thank you for trusting and growing me in ministry. Your leadership and guidance is invaluable and has indeed brought refinement in my life.
Bolanle and Ibrahim Morton, Saleem and Rahisha Wright, Donald and Wendy Williams, Allison Cosby, Richard Mitchell, and Annette Chesson, thank you for journeying with me, praying for me, keeping me accountable and challenging me to uphold the faith always.
To the members of Household of Faith Deliverance Worship Center thank you so much for all your prayers, love and support every thoughtful word and kind gesture has been appreciated.
To all my family and friends that I did not name please know that your contribution did not go overlooked or unnoticed. Thank you for taking the time to pour into me. I am blessed with a community that is unmatched.

www.ingramcontent.com/pod-product-compliance
Lightning Source LLC
Chambersburg PA
CBHW050113170426
43198CB00014B/2560